GW00859268

Eamonn Sheehy

SUMMER IN THE CITY STATE

STATE

Ceuta to Tangier Through Fortress Europe

Eamonn Sheehy

SUMMER IN THE CITY STATE

STATE

Ceuta to Tangier Through Fortress Europe

EAMONN SHEEHY

Eamonn Sheehy

Cover design by Derek Fitz,
Dark Buddha Art, Cork, Ireland.

Additional editing services by T.J. Sheehy.

Thanks to Susan MaierMoul and Niall Sheehy for the
discussions, debates and exchange of ideas.

Cover image: Café Al Manara,
Petit Socco, Tangier.

Migrate To The Fringe Publishing
www.migratetothefringe.com

CONTENTS

Summer…

From an idyllic archipelago on the Moroccan Mediterranean, 'Summer In The City State' takes a stirring trip through the little known Spanish enclave of Ceuta, on through Fortress Europe, and into the Rif cities of Northern Morocco.

Lyrical, reflective and bound in an immersive journalism style - the journey takes place against the backdrop of a contemporary Europe in crisis; recounted through vividly told vignettes and a series of affecting photography.

Sprinkled with moments of desperation and optimism, the road trip taps into the changing identity of people and place, in a fascinating region on the fault lines of North Africa and Southern Europe.

While subverting traditional forms of travel narrative, a pulsating rhythm and omnipresent tension bleeds through this quirky, lucid and sometimes dark nonfiction travel novella.

Migrate To The Fringe, 2016

Route

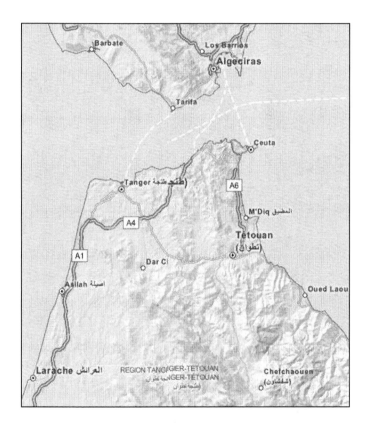

ALGECIRAS ~ CEUTA ~ TETOUAN ~ CHEFCHAOUEN ~ TANGIER ~ TARIFA

Eamonn Sheehy

Ceuta: Europe In Africa

GETTING HERE, THE BUS PASSED OVER THE SUNBURNT SKIN of Spain's Costa Del Sol; stopping in the resort cities of Malaga and Marbella to leave off flocks of pasty white tourists to enjoy the good life. Only a handful of people were left on board when we reached Algeciras. Many of them joined me as I walked the short distance to the port, where ferries depart for Africa. Algeciras takes its name from the Berber tongue, Amazigh - a script of striking visual flair that screams vibrancy, visible across most Berber areas of North Africa. Algeciras also stands as one of the main pillars bolstering Europe's Southern borders against the rest of the world. It is an integral part of modern day Fortress Europe, maintained by

'Frontex'; a major operation of surveillance and patrols that run along Europe's frontiers.

As the ferry departs, we pass fields of cargo containers stacked high along the port, carrying city names from across the world; Guangzhou, Danang, Marseille. The port is mega-sized; one of Europe's largest. Further out we pass the United Kingdom territory of Gibraltar as it juts out into the sea; an exclave of Queen and Country on the Spanish coast. This piece of little Britain on the Med mostly comprises of a large rock rising out of the sea; green foliage with the odd visible limestone patch, and an urban sprawl skirting around its waters edge. A band of clouds hover overhead like a protective halo. Spain wants it back, the British say no.

The lands of Europe fade away and the occupants of the ferry begin to take lunch up on deck. Some Spaniards in their later years talk loudly around a table of coffee and beers. On the upper deck, the speed of the ferry can be felt by those who wander up to take photos and gain a better view. The wind forces us back with gusto. A few young Moroccans take shade from the strong gale next to an engine room; seated on their haunches with shoes discarded around their chatting circle. From Algeciras to Ceuta, it is a short journey of 45 kilometres. It isn't long after the Spanish coast disappears when the African coast opens into view ahead. The coastline stands bare and hilly through the translucent haze of the warm afternoon. Clouds are draped low over Morocco's Rif Mountains. The landscape, in contrast to the Spanish coast, is stripped of any human infrastructure except for one point on the horizon – the city of Ceuta.

We taxi smoothly into the small, tidy port. Spanish accents gather by the ferry exit, joined by a few Moroccan families hauling an odd-sized selection of baggage. Across a single gangway, we all parade out into the heat; thirty degrees Celsius going on forty by the sweat on my back. No customs, no passport control. The surroundings still have a Spanish feel but prettier than the burnt up, overdeveloped coast of the Costa Del Sol. I was half expecting to embark into a cacophony of African urban, flanked by vast sand dunes and pockets of oversized alien green flora. But we haven't arrived in a new territory; this city state is still Spain. Technically, despite the shift in continent, this is still Europe.

Ceuta is placed beautifully on an archipelago. The city itself sits smack bang in the middle, elevated over pristine beaches that run along both its Atlantic and Mediterranean waters. Little villages are dotted around the modest coastline of twenty kilometres. Where the archipelago ends, Monte Hacho stands dominant over the stunning panorama, complete with its own military fortification. It is a hulk of rock that overlooks the city and the sea, and is a comrade of the Rock of Gibraltar. Both form ancient territorial markers known as the Pillars of Hercules; commonly called the Straits of Gibraltar today. In the Roman era, these pillars marked the ends of the known world. Myth has it that Hercules, while on his way to a mystical island, came before the Atlas Mountains. Instead of making the tough climb over, he smashed through them, leaving the pillars standing at each end.

As I walk into Ceuta, mopeds push up hills and walkers meander down steps towards the beaches. The city is clean and well laid out with green parks and pleasant streets. I stop on Calle Independencia, and look up at the tall apartment blocks facing the sea. Its balconies proudly overlook La Ribera beach on the Mediterranean. Palm trees run along at each side of me for as far as I can see. The beach, some fifteen feet below street level, is a comfortable cove of warm waters and clean sand. A volleyball game is at play. The girl poses to serve, as friends ready themselves for the volley. Swimmers bathe out into the blue sea as a lifeguard sits on a high chair in the white sands. The Moroccan coast winds around in front of us. I can almost make out the Moroccan town of Fnideq which is only 8 kilometres from here. Ceuta is calm and immediate in its beauty. Morocco wants it back, the Spanish say no.

In Ceuta's central Camoen's district, I leave my hotel and follow Paseo Del Revelin as it descends down to Plaza De la Constitucion; a central meeting point for Ceuta's avenues and residents. The people that grace the streets are predominantly Spanish with some Arab-Berber residents; although official figures say it is a fifty-fifty split. The whole exclave has a population of over eighty thousand people, meaning the city itself is compact and easy to explore. Three Arab women in traditional clothing walk past me on their way into a local indoor market. Spanish women and men stand outside the entrance selling lottery tickets. Inside the market, the usual selections of goods are available, as de rigueur for markets across Europe, but with a wider selection of fish dominating the stalls. Electrical goods are everywhere, much to the attraction of shoppers on holiday.

Ceuta is a tax-free zone. The city thrives on its tax exemption which propels a massive trade in every possible kind of merchandise between the sellers and the horde of buyers coming from neighbouring Morocco twenty minutes away. Every day from early morning, hundreds of traders come through the narrow border under special trading conditions. Local traders show identification as residents of the nearby Moroccan trading towns of Fnideq or Tetouan; and the near-undocumented trade flourishes. This generates huge profits for Ceuta and feeds the appetite of the Souks in Northern Morocco. Despite arguments over territorial sovereignty, Ceuta needs Morocco as much as Morocco needs Ceuta. Leaving the market I make my way to Plaza De la Constitucion. Here stands the giant bronze statue of Hercules himself. It is an impressive sculpture depicting human and mythical strengths, as primal brawn pushes the pillars apart. He stands high overlooking the Port of Ceuta. He seems to be eyeing a selection of luxury yachts, parked in rows to the left of the port. I quickly find a bus heading out of town along the Atlantic coast line.

Benzu is a Muslim village that looks out over the Strait of Gibraltar, where the Atlantic and the Mediterranean merge. After only minutes on the bus; it is a world away from Ceuta's downtown. Walking through the sleepy gathering of homes, I pass a tuck-shop where an elderly woman dozes inside. A Mosque ahead marks where the village ends. I cross the road to a little café called 'Musical'. It looks like a Mexican saloon from the outside. I order some mint tea and select some pastries from the gentleman at the counter. The Café sits on the cliff edge. From my table at the back, I look at the waves slam against the rocks below. Further down the grey coastline, I can see a large reinforced fence. It is the border fence between Ceuta and Morocco. This is where Europe meets Africa.

A little walk on from the café along a dusty road and I round a subtle bend where the frontier comes into full view. The vista is strikingly beautiful and rugged. But then the fence creeps into view - high shining metal cutting coarsely down through the foliage. The reinforced unnatural border runs from the rocky mountain top down into the sea. It is strange to see the fence cut the landscape deep down the middle. It has a tall lookout tower in the place where the road finishes. At the other side of the fence sits the Moroccan village of Belyounech.

Belyounech sits cosy in the cusp of Jebel Musa, or Mount Moses as it is called in English. In Ceuta, the mountain is known as 'The Dead Woman'. It looks like a female form laid out on her back, with her head resting in the sea. The sun comes down over Jebel Musa and sinks a slight distance off her forehead, slowly dipping into the silver Atlantic. As I stand there, cars drive straight up to where the road ends and then turn around; driving back in the direction they came. Beat up Golfs, dusty Mercedes and sparkling slick Minis. This is the evening ritual for the cruisers of Ceuta.

A man fishes off the rocks on the Ceuta side of the fence. I stand on the dust road overlooking him and the waves below. A small boat is slowly making its way ashore and some young boys run onto the beach to meet it. They pass out a line which is duly attached to the little raft. Then one of the stronger boys reels it in from a winch on the shore. Within a few minutes, I am joined by an old man, a local, curious to see what is going on below. "Buenos dias" he says as he shuffles up to the edge next to me and eagerly takes in the escapade below. A minute later a car eases up and parks next to us. The driver also takes a look at the boat below, which is now having its catch unloaded. Within ten minutes I have a little crowd around me; all of us looking downward onto the boat at the water's edge. Not a lot happens in Benzu on a Wednesday evening at the end of the road.

Benzu is an easy place to linger. You can sit, stare out at the sea and forget things. But time is ticking and by dusk, I begin to make my way back to the bus stop. It comes once an hour and on this last run of the day I am the only passenger. The bus pummels down the coast road towards Ceuta which is now a lit up reservation in the night. The driver is busy beeping everyone we pass. The evening walkers salute back. As driver and lone passenger weave around bends, unnerved, I grab onto the bar in front of me. The border crossing into Morocco, La Frontera is on the radio, and it sounds like trouble. As soon as I get back to the Camoen district, I take an evening tea in a café near the hotel. Locals sit around smoking, in a chorus of debate. The television has Ceuta's border on screen. Riot police shoot tear gas to repel several hundred migrants trying to rush the checkpoint. They form an armed barricade. The unrest looks capable of ripping the whole border open. Ceuta, despite its calm interior, has a people problem.

The morning heat wakes me early. At breakfast, the coffee servings are small, strong and coarse. The street hums with a flow of chatter that runs from Plaza De la Constitucion up past the hotel and onto

Ceuta's main square, Plaza De Los Reyes. Coffees and breakfasts fly out to customers seated at tables under parasols. A light summer rain begins to fall. I finish eating and take a walk. In the rain of Plaza De Los Reyes, what I see brings me to a sobering stop. On the footpath opposite are a row of tents, housing some families and sleeping bodies. Morning walkers pass on their way toward downtown. The tents are the fallout of a war some thousands of miles to the east. They are a protest against life in suspension. It is a camp by some Syrian asylum seekers sick of days in endless detention.

A blanket of multi-coloured fabric runs around the margins of the square. People are visible between the gaps. Some lay curled in sleep, others talk amongst themselves. The patchwork of materials shelter mostly families. The rain is stopping but the heat continues to rise. I read a Spanish slogan which is plastered across a large metal fence at the end of the tented settlement. 'Los Sirios, Quieren ir a Madrid, Ya aqui nos mantendremos. Hasta conseguir Neustros Objectivos'. Two Syrian flags and a large Spanish flag adorn the banner, with a hand painted love heart in the middle. Clothes hang drying across some rope. I see a young girl in her twenties sitting under a canopy looking out at me. I cease pointing my camera. Instead, she motions me to continue with an encouraging nod; and her hand does a sweep of the surroundings. Take photos, here, take photos of where we have ended up; our call for help. These Syrians are from the capacity-breached asylum centre in Ceuta. This is the asylum system of Fortress Europe. They are now stuck in Ceuta and can't go forward or back. The long and often lethal route from Syria to safety has led them to Europe. But the Europe they are looking for is across the Mediterranean. The banner translates as 'We Syrians want to go to Madrid to continue to pursue our aims. We haven't left a war to come to a prison.' City administration offices look down onto the square and its new hosts. People walk by the camp, as if not to see the desperation spread on the floor of their city. But of course, in modern day Europe, asking for help is complicated, wrapped tightly in red bureaucratic tape.

Leaving Ceuta town centre, the bus climbs an elevation overlooking the Mediterranean and carries on to the border with Morocco. Across the no-man's land between Spain and Morocco, stretches no less than three high fences topped with barbed wire and equipped with motion detectors, flood lights and automatic tear gas canisters. Over the years dozens have lost their lives trying to scale these fences to get into Spanish Ceuta, with the dreams of making it further to a life in Europe. This is La Frontera. It is the real frontier of Fortress Europe. The Mediterranean is the buffer zone. It is here that fences are stormed. It is also here where people die.

Fifteen alone died on the beach to my left months earlier; close to where the bus leaves us off. People were spotted by border officials swimming in from the sea. Shots were fired by police into the waves. Then some unknown bodies lay dead on the warm sand.

From the bus stop, I gingerly follow those ahead of me. Some struggle with large plastic bags, manoeuvring the narrow walkway leading through to the Moroccan side of the frontier. A high wall stands on my right and a metal fence on my left. Through this fence I can see a roadway blocked by barriers and border patrol officers. Passport control is a fluid affair. My passport is presented, stamped and I am waved onward. A little further and nearing the end of the tunnel, those ahead began to slow down. They are taking an avid interest in a drama unfolding beyond the metal bars on my left. I slow down. A group are being pushed back through the large metal gates, back into Morocco. There are around fifteen individuals; women and men, all possibly traders. A large border guard, with his head out and shoulders forward, shouts at the group. They shuffle away from him, back to the threshold of the frontier. Two officers are ready by his side, facing the irate gathering. Another border guard off to the side of the confusion looks on while gripping his baton with intent. I stop by the bars wanting to take a snapshot. I raise my small camera phone and covertly take a few crooked pictures.

The standoff still has everyone's attention. I figure I can take another few shots without being seen. This time I take my time and even the shot into frame; all within balance. Suddenly a large man from inside the fence starts to shout at me. His walking stick is raised in the air and he quickly comes in my direction. Fuck. I put the camera down and start to walk on towards the Moroccan exit.

"Hey you! Please stop! you!" I see an official identification tag around his neck. My heart begins to drum and my mouth dries up. He comes to the bars and asks my name.

"Eamonn".

"Where are you from Mr. Eamonn?"

"From Ireland, I am just on holiday."

I stand there hoping he would dismiss me; send me on my way. Over his shoulder I catch sight of the Moroccan traders, moving back quickly from the approaching blue uniforms ganging up on them, battle ready.

"Mr. Eamonn, would you like a short city tour of Tetouan? My name is Abdul. I am an official guide. I can promise you a professional tour. At a very good price."

I begin to walk off, somewhat relieved, but annoyed by this sly interruption. Abdul follows, coming out of the border to cut me off on the Moroccan side. After regaining my composure and sizing him up, I figure twenty euro isn't bad for a fast tour of Tetouan. And it makes getting a taxi to Tetouan hassle free.

"Okay Abdul, let's go."

A patchwork of blue taxis are parked tightly together on the hillside just beyond the border point. Rectangular rows of battered blue metal of varying shades sit melting in the sun waiting for passengers. The landscape is barren and sunburnt. The contrast is strong. In just a few steps, I have gone from a manicured and water-sprinkled Europe, into an altogether new and different place.

We sit into one of the blue taxis; me in the front passenger seat and Abdul shouting Arabic in the back. It is here I learn that Abdul is half deaf. He shouts up front to me and the driver. With a white hat, and wide Bono style sunglasses on an aged and stubble face; he takes up most of the backseat with his height and broad shoulders. A large hearing aid is wrapped around his right ear. He is dressed in a glowing white Jallaba and sandals. Slowly straining into position he groans, and shouts again at the young driver. The driver puts the Sedan into gear and we move off. Dust begins to rise yellow outside the driver's window. His long legs in threadbare, faded blue jeans, floor the pedals and he works up through the gears while gaining momentum towards Tetouan.

The car has no seat belts. The driver takes us down the highway at speed, overtaking car after car like a boy eagerly gaining points in a video game. I didn't mind, although I hold onto the dashboard and pray a little to my inner self for reassurance. We swayed from side to side, passing slow movers as we drive on. I wanted him to maintain the speed, but Abdul in the back was getting nervous and voiced a hoarse acidic objection. I looked over at the young man behind the wheel. He liked to drive fast; I could see that as he worked up through the gears. He soon gives in to Abdul and eases up on the speed. Abdul starts to settle down.

Tetouan

THE DRIVER TURNS UP THE MUSIC. A minuscule mp3 player is hooked up to the speakers. Cables, pinned down with black tape, snake across the dashboard. Algerian pop music blasts through the crackling outlets and sees us past Fnideq village on our right, and M'Diq beach resort on our left. I had hoped to walk from the border to Fnideq. When I stood on Ceuta's Calle Independencia, overlooking La Riberia beach and onto the shores of Morocco, I pictured myself walking along the dust road in the heat. A trek through the ripeness of the new and unknown. But now, here I was zooming past Fnideq in a car along the coast road that takes us speeding toward the large market town Tetouan.

"Take pictures! Take pictures!" urges Abdul. The tour has begun. I snap some photos of the roadway to keep him happy.

"I am professional guide, thirty years." he says. And Abdul proceeds to pass me some old photos from a fat Filofax to reassure me. Old 1970s and 80s shots of happy faces in the sun. All groups of random people in sunglasses. It could be anyone anywhere.

"I was their tour guide. Big bus tours!"

I give an impressed nod. We ease down the streets of Tetouan and the high stone walls of the Medina come into view. We pull up outside Bab Al Oqla; a centuries old gateway that leads through to the fortified old town which is made up of a confusing warren of houses and souks. I pay the driver. It takes Abdul a few minutes to escape the confines of the back seat. Then he is off up the steps with his walking stick; towering confidently above everyone else while I follow in tow behind him. Once through the old gateway, we stall intermittently at points of interest along the away. The mosque, the Jewish synagogue, the carpenter's workshop, the shoemaker, a shop where two young men painstakingly untangle a mess of metal wires. The stops are brief and Abdul's history lesson is bare. All I know is that Tetouan is a city founded by refugees fleeing Spain. The Medina is wholly authentic with little to no tourists around. Abdul knows everyone, and stops here and there to say hello and shake hands with neighbours. We arrive by some fruit stalls. Standing in front of the huge colourful array, I select some large shiny black dates from the spread. Abdul stands talking to the trader as I load up a plastic bag like a little boy foraging away in a tuck-shop. I quickly pay the trader, and Abdul waves me on to follow him.

Abdul I assume is a man who lives alone. Unkempt, it looks like half his breakfast has spilt down his front. The beard growth is erratic across a chin of dried food and flaky skin. We stride onwards, up towards the tanneries, passing Gaza Street on the way. Is it a signifier of the deep solidarity between Morocco and Palestine? Or does it come from a more direct translation of the Hebrew word Ghazza, meaning 'a strong place'? Appropriate when I consider we are walking through the Jewish quarter of old; Tetouan's 'Mellah' district.

The tour is swift. After the tanneries, Abdul leads me back down through Tetouan's maze of streets and before I know it, I am in a small taxi sweating with the midday heat. The car is bumper to bumper as it tries to bully through the thick city traffic. This time Abdul sits up front and I take in the street chaos from the back. We soon arrive at Tetouan bus station. Abdul turns to me, instructing I get a five coin ready to pay the minicab. We get out and the rush is on. Abdul walks frantically into the big building and I follow fast. He shouts back "Get a five coin for this man!" It seems the man is a local attendant ready to show me to the correct bus. I'm not quite sure what is meant to happen here. I drop the coin in his hand, and he shows me to the appropriate ticket window. As I pay for my ticket the freelancing attendant is urging me to hurry after him. Abdul is now in a spin in the middle of the station hall. He shouts again. "Fast! The bus!" I struggle with my wallet, pull my bag across my shoulder and follow Abdul out to the departure zone, leaving the attendant behind.

"The tour fee! And the tip!" he shouts again, practically pulling me forward through a crowd and out onto the bus quay. The pressure is on heavy. The bus in front of us looks full. I drop the notes in his hand and add a healthy tip. As soon I reach the top steps of the bus, Abdul is gone. Spinning like a tornado back to the border for another tourist.

The Quran Salesman

I PUSHED DOWN to the middle of the bus looking for a free seat. I found one by a window and a minute later, I was joined by a young local woman; her hands full of shopping bags. She sat down, gave me a bright smile, and then began to wedge her bags of vegetables in front of her legs. Subtly, she tried to force forward the seat in front of her. She then settled back with a portable radio and headphones, ready for the journey ahead. The bus driver stood outside in the dusty station yard, still directing passengers up the steps and sorting baggage for late-comers. There was no rush after all. Abdul's panic now seemed like a drill; pay up quickly and go. The bus waited for some time more and, when full, we pushed on toward Chefchaouen. The bus climbed the roadway through a wide and sunburnt landscape. The mountains rolled by in gradual climbs and inclines, and we stopped for the country folk of the Rif valley along the way.

The Quran salesman had the full attention of everyone on the bus. He got on at one of our brief stops. The bus rounded tight bends in trails of black smoke, and he held on firmly to an overhead handrail, while addressing everyone from the top of the bus. Then, walking the aisle in a mild rant of what I assume was Berber or a skewed Arabic dialect, he handed out pocket-sized Qurans to everyone except me. He gave me a glance before carrying on; seemingly deciding the book would serve a better purpose in the hands a neighbour.

Once back at the top of the bus, he ripped into a passionate recital. He read from the small book as if recounting a fantastic new revelation. Everyone around me focused on the scriptures, reading along out loud with the young man. In his brown slightly oversized suit, he held the bus captive. He was thin, and the white shirt was ill-fitting over his narrow shoulders. Within five minutes the reading came to an end. He then started to retrace the trail of Qurans down through the bus; this time collecting coins from their new owners. The woman next to me tucked the Quran into her vegetable bag with a pleased satisfaction; then dutifully retrieved some coins for the oncoming salesman.

All around me, the passengers were left in what could only be described as a 'bless'd' mood. The Quran salesman departed as fast as he arrived. Outside, he passed my window with a satisfied smile. He laid his suitcase on the gravel at the side of the road, and there he waited with a long shadow for the next bus, and onto the next pious pitch. Our bus, now a morally rejuvenated flock, continued uphill toward a mountain town known for its calm, and for a certain few, its cannabis-driven ambitions. Chefchaouen is out of the way; isolated in the heights of the Rif. As mountain towns usually go – fiercely independent and spirited - Chefchaouen is a relaxed affair. Prior to 1920, no foreigners were permitted behind its high walls. Nowadays, the locals still remain private and at a distance, but more appreciative of visitors. The initiated simply called it Chaouen.

Chefchaouen

IN CHEFCHAOUEN, the air is warm and dry. Clear blue skies peer down on the days I spend wandering this high-walled town in Morocco's Rif Mountains. Drinking mint tea and smoking Kif, I watch the evening sun slowly drop as the town becomes sleepy. Feeds of succulent Lamb Tagine home-cooked in cute hotpots followed by more Kif. Time moves on a different level here; there is no European living against the clock. Chefchaouen is the blue city of the Rif. Small stone homes are huddled along whitewashed alleyways, all painted in calming shades; Azure, Maya and Powder blue.

I stand on the hotel balcony at the end of the night, looking out over the mountain range. It is a plateau of silence, only broken by jangling bells as mountain goats scramble along slopes that hug the north side of town. In the darkness to the east lies the town of Ketema. A no-go zone with Hashish markets and a lawless reputation, it's one of Europe's main sedative sources. I imagine armed wholesalers cruising in SUVs, buying hash in bulk to feed the demand on the streets of Europe. But ancient Chefchaouen captivates. This is the real world. I fall back into my bed and the sound of the night reverberates in my head while I fade to sleep.

The bus pulls into the depot and the few of us waiting pile on up the steps. The driver takes my ticket money and I take a seat. We slowly leave Chefchaouen on our way to the pulsating city of Tangier on Morocco's north-western corner. From the slowness of rural Morocco to an African urban hybrid, Tangier is a pressure cooker. Here is the merger of those trying to survive, trying to profit, and trying to escape. So many people with cross-section motives fill its winding alleyways.

The bus labours downhill towards the tail end of town, where we stop to pick up a much larger crowd. Two Policemen holding rifles quickly board the bus. They scan the interior and usher everyone down to the last few rows. The bus driver reassures us that all is okay. Then a chain line of prisoners board one after another and fill every seat on the bus. The hot afternoon sun washes in through the windows. The chained - all men - are joined by a few women, who I presume are either wives or mothers. They carry food and bottled water in plastic bags. A policeman takes station up front and we start again, driving down the Rif Mountains, through the valley and towards Tetouan on route to Tangier.

One prisoner sits slumped in defeat. It's like the atmosphere has been suddenly ripped from the sky above. It came out of nowhere. There is no sun, only a sullen, heavy grey hanging over his head. Thoughts on how to deal with the oncoming sentence have overthrown him, and a mild panic sets in. A piece of bread touches his lips and he looks slowly down to the hand of his wife. She hides half crouched in the aisle, trying to stay out of the Guard's view while feeding her shackled husband some food.

We reach Tetouan a few hours later. Some prisoners who had fallen asleep are now waking to nudges. Faces are fixed to glass while the bus reverses in-between two tall concrete pillars, further into what I now assume is a prison yard. Looking out the front window, I can see locals stopped across the street. They stand looking at the bus and it's chained up cargo as we roll back to a standstill.

The prison enclosure contrasts dramatically with the blue Moroccan vista above its towering walls. In the yard, armed men create a partition from the street and a channel to the prison. The shackled column is herded from the bus into the building. A guard stands between us and those departing, while the wives stay seated -- watching their loved ones slip away. The chained men look back, worried. The yard leads to an endless rotation of days and nights, all between walls that get narrower over time. The bus starts up again, and the prison doors close behind us.

In Tangier

JUST AFTER WORLD WAR ONE, the era of the international zone saw Tangier ruled by a coalition of different countries. The tough port city, with its old towering Kasbah standing steeply on the very north-western edge of the African continent, looks roguishly across to Spain, and serenely out to the wide Atlantic. Throughout its history, Tangier has worn the black flag of piracy, the green and red of Portugal and has been draped in the restraints of the British Empire. The International era from 1924 saw eight parties rule the city; including the Spanish and French whose deep cultural influence is in evidence today. It became one of the most notorious city states in the world. It attracted the most leftfield, outsider personas. In a vacuum of anything and everything, Tangier was the answer for a litany of abstract characters. It became a playground for the clandestine and exiled in the mid-1900's - a haven for the illicit and a sanctuary from a stagnating life in Europe. It all ended in 1956. Once Tangier was handed back to Morocco, the King was determined to lead the city toward a more controlled Islamic code of ethics. When the Islamists began to flex their muscles, a lot of westerners left town. The party was over. The 'years of lead' had now arrived, and quickly tamed any wild flames across the city.

*

I had walked into the contents of someone's stomach. Puke, in a pulpy mosaic, spread out at both sides of my feet. I bent over to dig my bag out of the luggage hold. I stepped back from the bus to leave the swell retrieve their belongings and stamped my feet in the hot dust to clear off the slippery gunk. I was going uptown, but I wasn't exactly sure where uptown was. I started off towards Tangier's beach front.

Avenue Mohamed VI runs for a mile along the clear sands of Tangier's beach area. Cafés and hotels sit along the city side of the avenue. The shade of the footpath wins me over and I cross the road, then pass the Rif and Marco Polo hotels. Now nearer to the port, I take a street upwards away from the beach, following the city as it climbs uphill.

At the bottom of this incline stands a local man. The sun has me zoned out and lethargic. He has me standing by his side before I know it.

"Hey, how are you? You want to buy? I have this, it's amazing."

I look down, thinking dope, drugs. With caution, I check his hands. All he has is a large rock form in his outstretched palms.

"Take a look."

The rock is granite grey and rough. It sits split open in his hand. The inside reveals striking purple crystals. I stare at it for a minute. He smiles with bad teeth, looking down into the rock in dreamy content. Crystals sparkle in a liquid purple, shining up at us; trails of fuzzy pink spread across the interior flesh of the rock. I snap out of my sun stroked stupor, pass on the sale and move on towards uptown, leaving him to his protestations behind me. I was mystified. Was it a hunk of purple crystal or a breed of exotic shellfish?

Finally, I find the hotel. The Hotel Rembrandt has a heavy aura of nostalgia. The day's travel is stuck to me in a mesh of dust and sweat. Travel's magic powder. My room on the first floor has a balcony. It looks out onto Boulevard Pasteur. This is the pulse of central Tangier. It is reminiscent of the impressive, grand districts of inner-city Paris. Clean but chaotic, Boulevard Pasteur is flanked by cafés and shops. Alive into the late hours with transient shoppers and stationary street life; it's definitely a spin into the unknown.

Lying on my bed after an afternoon shower, the midday swelter has me breathing heavy. Eyes half shut, I stare at the curtains of the balcony. They are thick and smooth, and sway lightly in the breeze of the open doors. I listen to the sounds that drift in. The sound of urban North Africa. All cities sound different. This is the sound of Tangier breathing. The whizz of traffic passes like clockwork and the hum of large saloons, white robust Mercedes, motor on by. The rat-a-tat of the three-wheeled trikes; little rickety trailers attached. The loud straining of lorry engines, tugging heavy loads and spurting smoke into the tall street. The small, primed buzz of bubble cars speeding through town and slowing to a stop. Then it all stops. The traffic lights pull everything in, and broadcasts its high pitched clatter for exactly thirty seconds. I drift into a lull, but I'm pulled back out when the motorised collective starts up again. The rollercoaster goes on. The city air. The heat. Water drips in taunt rhythmic drops from the silent corner at the other end of the room, into the ceramic washbowl where a few patient mosquitos sit static.

In the reception area, the air conditioning zooms, blasting out cool air, and new guests come in from the sun-bleached street outside. The grand reception desk dwarfs the attendant inside it. He stands in front of a panel of leather tagged keys. He looks at the paperwork strewn out in front of him with a consumed expression. It is too warm to go out. The hotel bar is quiet. I settle in a high chair with a view across the lounge and out onto the street.

"A beer please."

The barman nods back, pulls me a drink and offers me a cigarette. He is your classic hotel barman, easy going and unobtrusive.

The street that runs down the side of the hotel is narrow and slopes towards the beach. A little van backs down uncertain, starting and stopping, to the instructions of two men shouting directions with erratic hand actions. I walk past the confused driver and his cohorts, and continue around to the back of Hotel Rembrandt. Standing on some broken steps, I look down at a rubbish strewn piss-stained alley. A steep incline of steps run down old Rue Magellan. On the slope where the steps end and the road begins, a man lays stretched out on the footpath. He has a bag tucked under his head and a cap over his eyes. His hands, browned from the sun, are placed across his chest while he sleeps. The Tangier Inn is two steps beyond him. Its sign stands out on the street where not much else lives. Across the road, men work into the evening, pounding the walls of a house into rubble. I take the narrow doorway into the bar.

This evening all is calm and quiet in the Tangier Inn. No unhinged or 'out-there' guests are tearing up the establishment and I have a slow drink. The clientele barely notice me sitting in the corner. Attached is the Hotel El-Muniria, where Burroughs wrote his mind-bending chaos novel 'The Naked Lunch'. Walking the streets of Tangier in the 1950's, William Burroughs – an American writer, junky and homosexual - stood out as a dark foreign hustler. Shooting holes in walls of rented rooms, scoring drugs, partners and stories in the chaos of urban Africa. He lost his mind and ran wild through imagination. Then the Beat writers, Ginsberg and Kerouac turned up, to pull Burroughs back into shape, and get his Naked Lunch off the hotel floor and into the hands of Olympia Press in Paris.

Back out on the street all is calm. The destructors have gone home and the sleeper has scattered. All I am faced with are two large rats as I walk back up Rue Magellan. At the top of the steps, on the right against the dead grey wall, they both stand staring down on me. I stall for a minute and take a step forward. Then one of them scurries across to the other side of the footpath, as if marking an indisputable boundary. Large and steadfast, both stare down at me like muggers in a ghetto waiting on my next move. The Rembrandt stands tall in the dusk behind them.

Eamonn Sheehy

Les Insolites

JUST ACROSS FROM THE HOTEL, the Librairie Des Colonnes is open on Boulevard Pasteur. It remains one of the most iconic bookshops in North Africa. The morning is warm and balmy. After breakfast, with eager steps, I cross from the Rembrandt over to the historic bookshop. Its shelves are stuffed with the reverential; from highly respected Tangier authors to their international counterparts. Portraits of Mohamed Choukri and other Moroccan writers look down on me from a height. The shop is intimate. Like a private library in a grand mansion, it is a wordy almost solemn space. The legacy this shop has, both as a bookseller and a publishing house, is staggeringly dense. Francis Bacon held one of his first art exhibitions here. Truman Capote, Jack Kerouac and a litany of other literary outsiders paid frequent visits. I harangued the gentleman at the counter for some Driss Ben Hamed Charhadi in English. His novel, 'A Life Full of Holes', recounting a harsh life amid the cultural collisions of Tangier in the early 1900s, had me floored. Once sorted, I left happy and another Tangier curio unveiled.

But who were the pens rewriting the rulebook in today's literary landscape? Morocco today is in flux and its literary challenges are ever-present. These kind of questions led me back across a busy Boulevard Pasteur and down a nearby side street called Rue Khalid Ibn Oualid. Here is where Les Insolites is based. The street dips slowly toward the Medina and the sea. And the shop sits on the right-hand side.

Les Insolites. The insolent, the bold, the daring? The unusual. It is known as a bookshop with a difference, on a bold quest towards literary and artistic progression in Tangier. The doors open into a bright airy space and I can see the shop is sectioned into various focal points of expression. Freshly framed watercolours take up one section of wall. The artist has created a series of half obscured human motifs, light fragile body forms; Moroccan creativity laid bare in an expression of fresh colour and emotion. At the back, a man is busy arranging new book arrivals out of boxes. Bright photography pieces are mounted on the other wall. The mix of street and landscape photography can only be unique to

Morocco's otherworldly regions south of Tropic of Cancer's 23rd degree parallel. These works by photographer Delphine Melese, depict life beyond Marrakech and into the Saharan territories, where human life goes to a slow, and everything turns to red dust and yellow.

The shopkeeper had finished his arranging, and not before long we were talking about life in Tangier. He introduces himself as Cedric.

"Here, life is definitely different from Europe; a lot quieter. There is no pressure to go out or anything. Here you can learn to be comfortable with yourself. It's very different from Paris, where I'm from." He cradles a small slumbering baby in his arms.

"Stephanie and I both run Les Insolites" adds Cedric, raising his head towards his partner who is speaking with a customer at the front of the shop.

The sun floods in through the large window and washes the floor beneath their feet with a blinding brightness. I ask for some recommendations. Cedric starts pulling out some titles for me; all the while holding his child in his other arm.

"Here is Taia Abdellah, a gay man who has adapted to a writing career in Paris. Telling stories of homosexual awakening in Morocco, through Arabic or Maghrabi, is still taboo today. Taia is pushing the boundaries.

Abdelhak Serhane's 'Les Enfants des Rues Etroits' – this is a scathing literary description on social issues and the human condition, specific to Morocco's poor under the Hassan II regime. He is a renowned writer on a classic scale.

Fouad Laroui's 'Du Bon Usage Des Djinns', he is an economist and a storyteller of immense talent. A coarse wit reflecting on religion, immigration and the human struggle in Morocco.

Rita El Khayat is a towering Nobel Prize nominee from Rabat. She is a prolific and challenging writer, exploring female issues in Morocco and the representation of the woman in the Arab world."

The list goes on and the books pile up on the table, as Cedric and I delve into other writers from varying realms from the socio-political to the poetic. For these more daring Moroccan writers, to freely express themselves comes through the prism of translation. The books in front of me are all in another language; French and Spanish. Once they are not in Arabic or Maghrabi, it seems the Moroccan censors aren't troubled too much. And the stories flow. But access to such stories mean readers must have the education to read French or Spanish; not a typical trait in a Morocco still plagued with illiteracy.

Stephanie approaches us. Also from France, she has lived in Tangier for five years. In a short time, she has built Les Insolites into a bookshop, art gallery and a public space for literary discussions. Today she is preparing for a book launch and signing taking place later in the evening.

"I was just telling Eamonn about some of the contemporary writers Morocco has." says Cedric. Stephanie, a beautiful and confident young woman, has the artistic vision of their enterprise very much on the path forward.

The contemporary features heavily on the shelves of Les Insolites. I want to know what they think of the bohemia that hijacked Tangier's literary landscape for decades and still dominates current literary perspectives on the city. "You have William Burroughs here too." I say to Stephanie, gesturing towards a copy of old Bill in French, looking up at us from a table nearby.

"Les Insolites isn't just a bookseller selling copies of Bowles, Burroughs and Williams," she replies. "Sure, we have the old Tangier literary bunch available, but we are more focused on the writers of today. The writers emerging at this very exciting time in Morocco...we want them to be read and to be recognized for what they do. These writings are the real barrier breakers in today's literary climate." she says as she draws her hand across the selection of novels laid out in front of me.

"We are trying to show that Moroccan and North African contemporary writers can evoke danger and extremely progressive ideas; even more so than their international contemporaries."

This is a breath of fresh air to hear. The old scene of Tangier, layered in nostalgia, although still intriguing to me, is truly well-fed. The selection of writers on the table in front of me, and the high calibre of their craft, is overwhelming. I reach out for a copy of Abdellah Taia's 'Salvation Army'.

Eamonn Sheehy

ACROSS
THE STRAITS

CEUTA

Standing in Benzu. A man casts his fishing rod from the rocks. Belyounech sits cosy in the cusp of Jebel Musa at the far side of the European border fence ~ the separation between Morocco and Spain; Europe and Africa.

City Side

Beach Side

TETOUAN

CHEFCHAOUEN

The sun creeps in over Jebel El Kalaa. The Kif is
oily soft and rolls like clay.

TANGIER

From the Medina and in through the old arches, you emerge out onto the sun drenched pavements of the Grand Socco. The sweetheart of Tangier.

Laid out on a warm Rue Magellan

William The Guide

HE SAID HIS NAME WAS WILLIAM; not a very Moroccan name I thought. He is one of the false 'guides' that roam the Medina; the old walled section of town. The narrow alleys form a confusing labyrinth. As I walked, he followed closely. I was trying to reach Café Hafa - a café perched on a reputable viewing point overlooking the Atlantic. I knew I was heading in the right direction. Then old streets started to split off all around, with v-junctions breaking to the left and the right. Tiny windows looked down on the pathways leading on and on; hinting little to where I was heading. 'No thanks' wasn't working as an answer to William's persistent offers. He knew well I didn't have a clue where I was. So we agreed a few euro for the 'tour'. Like others, he is just trying to stay afloat. His company also served to keep other opportunists at bay. I still remained wary.

Walking down a narrow street, I caught sight of some eyes peering at us through half-opened doors. Another group of them stood cautiously together, looking out from a smaller alley further on.

"Hey William, who are those people looking out from the alleyways?" I asked.

He walked a few steps ahead, then slowed down and murmured back in almost a whisper, "They are waiting for the boats, to Europe. "They are black Africans. They are not like us."

'They are not like us'. As William hints, Moroccans are distinctive from what he calls 'black Africans'. The descendants here are mostly of Arab and Berber origin; like the majority across North Africa's coast; from here to the East through Algeria, Tunisia, Libya, and Egypt.

Stories on the streets of Tangier have moved to the very same 'they' William nods towards; a very different type of visitor than myself. Migrants and Refugees. They come in from the greater Maghreb. They are here after gruelling journeys through unforgivable landscapes; vast deserts and huge mountain ranges. They come from a variety of regions across Africa – Mali, Niger, Cameroon, Senegal, Sudan. Through Ceuta and Tangier, they plan to move on across the Bay of Gibraltar toward

Europe. And now, like the refugees of Ceuta's town square, those fleeing the Syrian and Libyan regimes are vying for a place on the smugglers boats. We pass some more - the new clandestine of Tangier and northern Morocco; stigmatised and criminalised as dangerous migrants, a 'problem', a 'threat'. Europe crudely pays Morocco to police the exterior of its fortified fences across Northern Africa, keeping out these same people that watch me pass by. They have an impossible fight on their hands.

William has me sitting in a large open room. A man is rolling out a large expanse of carpet, then another and yet another. I was lost earlier in the street, but I feel really lost now. "How about this one?" says the carpet seller. "Feel that eh, feel, feels good eh?" he offers me the corner of a thick rug. I rub it between my fingers, half wishing for that magical puff of air that would instantly snap me back out onto the street.

"Nice.   It's nice and thick." I respond half deadpan.

"Sorry, I'm really not interested in carpets. I really have to go now."

But another rug gets spread. My attention is again directed to the detail and immersive hard work gone into creating it. William sits back on the sideline, watching me watching the seller. And the seller watches me back. And that was it for me and William. Just down from the carpet shop, we had it out. A loud protest over the ten euros I was paying him. It seemed it wasn't enough. He didn't like it. Some cursing. His hands flew into the evening air in anger. And mine flew even higher. Holding it at the tenner, we stingingly parted company. A bit pissed off at the whole rigmarole, I found myself at one of those cafés where minds come to meet.

Café Central is quiet this evening. A thinking café in the Petit Socco. And an off-kilter tourist haunt. I sat drinking tea in the shadows for an hour, just inside the main window, like a still life. Two guys chatted while watching the sports on the big screen. An old man in black shades sat in the corner. He shouted at random, in what I think was a mix of Spanish and Arabic. Sometimes the waiter, going from table to table changing ashtrays, shouted back. Other times the shouts formed a lone reassurance to his pale elderly self. We looked at each other for a bit. Then he shouted some more.

My seat by the window looks out onto the little square, once a small market and a main economic hub in Tangier. A woman at a table reads a book just outside the window, with a coffee by her side. Scooters and traders pass up and down, and locals hurry by on their way to the mosque for evening prayer. The street lights come on, still faint. It is getting dark.

Café El Manara across the street starts to fill up quickly. I presume the coffee there is cheaper or the

Café Central is too much a tourist lay-by for some of the locals. A man sitting at a small table outside El Manara lights a clay pipe and then cleans his table with a swipe of his arm. His face bares the rough skin of a hard rural life. He has a thick knotted beard and white tufts of scraggly hair hang stern over his bright eyes. He is brown from the sun with clothes frayed and faded.

The waiter drops a drink on his table; a steaming tea. And the man, supping on his pipe, starts giggling to himself amid the smoke reams floating around him. Within a few minutes, he is hunched over; convulsing in laughter. Then he takes another puff from the long clay pipe realm, leading deeper into the funny side of his imagination. Looking out onto the street, he offers rambling words to passers-by through the smoke clouds. More laughter breaks through his glassed out eyes. It's a scene that belongs in absurdia, and I can't help but laugh along with him as the day comes to an end.

The Great Unease

WHEN I AWOKE, my oversized bedroom was painted in a bright coat of orange. The sun shone through the balcony doors and penetrated the thick curtains. The street noise flooded my ears and my head decompressed as I got out from underneath the covers. And there in my room, I pottered around for some hours, suspended in my own time. I shaved and washed. On the TV in the corner, the Arabic news reads out a chatter of background noise. I choose a light shirt to wear and then lumbered over a map of the city.

From the Rembrandt, I took a quiet side street down towards the Medina. It wore a warm blanket of brilliant white, as the sun rose for midday. The Hotel Continental sat off to the left of the port. I could see it in the distance across the scattered roofs of the

Medina. Its sign perched high in the air with the sea beyond; a beacon signalling lost foreigners as they navigated the riddle of alleyways in the old town. At the end of the street, the footpath opened out into a small park, with steps that ran steeply down to the Medina. The park was in silence and an old man sat against a tree, looking down on Tangier bay below. From here he could see the slow movements of vessels crossing the busy port. The tree was a comfortable base for him to sit; hidden in the shade from the midday sun. It offered the perfect viewing point to see who was coming his way. It gave him the chance to size up those who warranted attention. This was after all, work. And there was no point dabbling in acts of persuasion with a passer-by who was without certain, going to stonewall you. It's no easy job; the hustle. And today, I wasn't going to make things any easier for him.

I was in off form. I walked with an urgency; with a short and impatient temper. I could see him waiting for me, despite his modest placement, for that smooth interjection on the passing wanderer. Half sour, I felt like bait on the street.

"Hey friend..." he started.

I started to tense up and slowing down to meet him I said "What do you mean 'friend'?" My voice began to rise. I continued.

"I'm not your friend" - the word 'friend' carried a prolonged twisted spike.

"Hey sorry young man, I just…"

I cut him off. The heat of rage was building up.

"I am not a friend; I'm not a nice guy."

The old man gasped out some empty words. He looked genuinely confused and puzzled.

"You looked like a nice guy." he said in a reasoning tone.

"But I am NOT." I returned in a shout.

I was now becoming aware of the surrealism of the moment - flipping out on an old man sitting by a tree in a park in Tangier. A dead heat coming from my belly. A deranged mix coming from my mouth. With an arched back, I looked down on him, seated low against the tree. His hands rested on his knees. A round plump belly underneath a tired looking t-shirt and an aged face topped with light grey hair carefully combed across a forehead before disappearing under a comfortable brown cap.

He looked back at me, cowered and bewildered, as if my eyeballs had bulked out and turned liquid black before him. The strangled ball of stress tensed hard in my stomach. I walked away, already seething with regret.

Atelier Des Italiens

IT WAS LIKE THE SUN WAS CHAINED TO MY BACK. With a streaming brow and soaked shirt, I struggled up Rue De La Kasbah. Once inside the northern gate of the Kasbah, I followed the alleyways, narrow and cool in the midday shade, which are constantly kept spotless by local residents. They were a whitewashed maze, and now became the scene of hide and seek for local children.

I was on my way to Atelier Des Italiens; a small gallery of mixed media art run by two Italian artists, Dario Iosimi and Laura Li. I wanted to feed my fascination with a more contemporary flavour of leftfield Tangier. The confined space was hidden deep in the Kasbah; where ideas and art were nurtured, shaped and spirited to life. I had found them on the internet before my arrival. It was not a public gallery of art, but a home hosting a workspace and display. The work looked intriguing and the invitation for those wishing to see it was open upon contact. I was enthusiastically welcomed.

The front door leads me into a cool breezy front lounge with minimal yet voluptuous furnishings. A beautiful portrait of an elegant Greta Garbo in lavish dress and a jewelled clasp poses the height of one wall. She holds back an emerald green curtain revealing an aqua blue mosaic; a dominant trait of Moroccan art. Gracefully suspended from the ceiling of the intimate space are the large 'Hands of Fatima'; beautiful creations crafted with a protective, positive symbolism, and designed from a special resin formulated by Atelier Des Italiens. The art pieces have the aesthetic of Moroccan retro and modern pop art. The sharp detail and clean almost see-through effect of each are refreshing. It feels like I have walked into some kind of dream gallery in the clouds.

In this front room gallery, I sit with both artists, getting a private tour of the creative process. Dario is a middle-aged man with a youthful energy. He reminds me of an Italian rocker of my own age. He wears a trucker hat, and with an unmistakably Italian animated flair as he tells me where it all began.

"I met Laura in Calcata, a bohemian village just north of Rome. We worked together there, on an art magazine in 2008. Then we collaborated on other projects like music festivals while still working on art. It was an artistic commune, a very creative place."

Laura sits across from me on a lounger, listening to her partner recount their journey.

"We moved to Morocco in 2010 and it has been a big change for us. But our artwork has progressed for us both since we came to Tangier." he continues.

Dario stands in front of me. I look up from a low sized seat, while he passionately explains the concepts behind Atelier Des Italiens artwork.

"The connections in our art are both traditional and modern, and yes technology is part of that creative process."

The creation of images using modern technology is interesting. I slightly associate some modern methods as an artistic betrayal, for some nonsensical reason. But this technological ingredient is a nectar considered integral and positive to Atelier Des Italiens.

"We have a passion for creating. This is the passion which drives all art. To be an artist you have to be open; if you are not open then you cannot create."

Laura creates a lot of the large prints and art cards that are displayed around Atelier Des Italiens, or 'The Italian's Studio' when translated into English. The prints show scenes of Ibn Battuta and Paul Bowles, against fantastic backdrops of the Petit Socco, the

Kasbah, and nearby Asilah. Vintage Maroc. The decadent Maghreb. The sensual and timeless. I take in the selection, picking out the scenes of people and place. Dario then suggests I stay for lunch. I accept with gratitude and Dario retreats to the kitchen to get something rustled up.

Laura has a similar alternative presence to Dario. Independently minded as most good artists are. Edgy and offbeat. I ask Laura what she makes of Tangier.

"Tangier is very inspirational. The light of the city is fantastic. You have seen the Grand Socco, the souks, and the people. These scenes inform a lot of the prints I create. We love it here," then she adds "We will have lunch on the terrace, you will love the views."

I follow the steep winding stairs that circumvent the tall narrow house. More artworks grace the walls of the stairway; a mixture of mosaic and paintings. Dario and Laura are in the kitchen preparing the salad. They urge me to continue my wander up onto the roof. The roof terrace has shade from the midday sun, with a table and chairs. The walls of the terrace are chest high and the Kasbah streets below slither confusingly between homes stacked tight together. The pavements are draped in a mix of dark shadows and sun-blasted light. One street brightly runs off down to the sea below and the whole bay shimmers blue. At the other side of the terrace, I can see a green park with some twisted, arching trees. Roofs with rusted satellite dishes are everywhere to be seen. And rows of sheets flutter in the wind, drying on a cross-tangle of clotheslines.

Throughout the decades, many people have come from abroad and made their homes on the fringes of Tangier. They reside in palatial Marshawn, overlooking the Atlantic coast, and along the fringes of Boulevard Pasteur where they can look down into the melting pot of the Medina and Kasbah. But it is few who have braved the transition to the inner sanctum of the Kasbah. Traditionally a tight-knit, hard living, closed off section of the city; it has never contained many outsiders. In fact, up to recent times, most foreigners wouldn't stand a chance here come nightfall. Wanderers would be out of the Kasbah before dusk, or risk the dangers of its winding alleyways.

Dario and Laura know only too well how difficult getting settled in Tangier is for artists. We take to the shade and to our lunch.

"It hasn't been easy. Tangier isn't an 'easy' place." laughs Dario. "The romantic ideal... the artistic foreigner, living the free life of luxury in Tangier...does not exist. There is still chaos. But chaos has its balancing attributes right?" he smiles.

We talk on and some hours later, Dario walks me down through the Kasbah. Café Baba comes into view on our right, another iconic drop out zone of bohemian cool, that can only be found in this alter-terrestrial city. Baba recently seeped back into the counter culture psyche through Jim Jarmusch's movie 'Only Lovers Left Alive', where ailing vampires Tilda Swindon and John Hurt sipped blood under anonymity, aided by kindly locals. The selecting by Jarmusch of Tangier as the cloaked, old world hideaway from the new world decay of Detroit is no accident. The dark romantic allure is strong around the alleyways of the Kasbah. Dario sees me off at Tangier's front door, Bab El Bhar; an old half crumbling, proud archway looking out over the blue Atlantic and across to the headlands of Spain. And we say our goodbyes.

Walking back through the Petit Socco and up to the Grand Socco, the streets are pulsating with evening shoppers. Near the gateway of the Medina that leads into the Grand Socco a trader sells balloons. The large and transparent articles have rice inside. And the trader shakes them into an ambient backdrop of sound that fills the whole street. The rice-rattle is trance-like. The voice of the shouting trader repeats calls projecting the specials of the day. A smattering of passing voices fall into this live improvisation in passing. Then I am out into the openness of the Grand Socco.

Man Boulevard Pasteur

THE SUN BLAZED across the cobbled street and into the big square. It splashed out across trader stalls, onto torn boxes and stacks of cardboard, and onto the legs of young men who were stretched out dozing on the grass. This is the epicentre of Tangier. Instantly recognizable, it is the true heart of the city and attracts all walks of life. The traders bring their produce from the countryside and circle the square with their stalls. The coffee drinkers fill the footpaths watching the shoppers. The wealthy of Marshan cross here to go to the fish market inside the Kasbah walls. The residents of the Kasbah cross here on their way to the Post Office up on Pasteur. Workers at the port pass here on their way to the docks.

Half worn from the sapping sun, I climbed on towards Boulevard Pasteur. Boulevard Pasteur felt cooler. The tall French colonial buildings shade one side of the street and I walked down the other with a bag swaying in one hand, trudging the last few lengths to my hotel.

This is where I encountered the hustler. I'll call him 'Man Boulevard Pasteur'; a stranger.

"Hello Mister do you remember me?!" he shouted, still midway across the road.

He tried to maintain a large smile; traffic skirting his heavy bulk. His attempts to reach me in the face of oncoming traffic were comic and increasingly unnerving. After he had my attention, I watched him for a good half a minute while I walked. He took lines of evening traffic in his stride. Like an overweight ballet dancer trying to hold grace. While sidestepping some moving cars his determined eyes stayed on me.

His large upper body suggested a man of considerable strength. Possibly in his mid to late fifties, he did not strike me as Moroccan; maybe French or Spanish. Despite the heat, he wore a great big bomber jacket; all greased up in a dirty dark blue. It was zipped tightly around him, like an outer skin for the street.

"I work in your hotel! Mister!"

He was panting heavily and now on the footpath next to me. A plump, sweaty face with a big grinning smile. He seemed to try on a few different smiles, registering which one worked best. He continued walking beside me as if we were friends who knew each other. Trying to fool some naive sod out of a few coins in order to eat - I could see his point. What are your options when trying to stay on the shaking side-car of life? He looked tired. An old timer. A tired, heavy hitting old timer.

Who really was this elaborate façade of a forgotten friend? He possibly lived a life alone. Homelessness, addiction, violence; trying to straddle any passing opportunities. A life excluded through poverty. He trudged through the streets, on endless rounds around the city, faced with the constant spectre of life on the fringes. Feeling like a fugitive, never in the ascendancy.

"You don't know me? I am staff in your hotel, the Rembrandt!" His words began to weigh on him. They started to shed and the false sincerity showed up in the lines he spun. From this weak delivery emerged the failure of the whole façade. It was now plain for us both to see.

Still walking, and without saying anything, he smacked his lips nervously in the humidity of the late evening. I could feel his anxiety fraying just steps away from me.

"Sorry, we don't know each other."
I couldn't think of anything else to say. Frustrated, he looked out of ideas and out of steam. I upped my pace and broke eye contact. And he resolved to do

the same. He headed off down a solitary side street. A shadow breaking onto a grey unwashed wall. A shadow sinking into a footpath pockmarked with depressions and crumbling.

Bar Number One

BAR NUMBER ONE HAS SINATRA'S 'MY WAY'
crooning through its small embryonic cocoon as I
enter. The lights are low. Candle shadows dance on
the walls, rousing to life the pictures of Tangier
cultural icons and esoteric art which hangs
throughout the bar. Three high tables sit by one wall,
and I take a seat at one of them. The bar itself sits
opposite, with space enough in-between for someone
to pass. Despite the cosy confines, the waiter still
'waits' on me. He is an old wholesome character and a
man with a warm approach. I ask for a beer. He softly
passes my order to the barman just steps away. A
minute later, again by my side, he hands me a cold
bottle. Bar Number One looks out onto Boulevard
Pasteur through open bay windows. A hive of activity

is visible all the way up the Boulevard toward Place De Faro. Streams of people flow up and down, ant-like, entering and exiting shops and taking seats outside cafés. The night sky spreads wide above the city - a sweeping canopy of dense chrome. Streaks of pitch black cut through the starry grey. Dark chasms sink way out into space.

The barman takes a high seat by the window and lights a cigarette. 'Comfortably Numb' begins to sound over the stereo. An instrumental. As it lifts, the black suited waiter fills out the chorus with some soulful humming. Toothless with age and gums on show, he serenades the bar while cleaning down tables. The barman likes to take in the city through the large window. He remains hard on the people who walk passed outside. A canon of jumbled street noise filters in through the window as he talks.

"The population has soared. A million people live in Tangier now, compared to fifteen years back. People have come in from the countryside, to work on the new port. The city has changed. I go fishing to get away from it all." he gestures to the mass of people flowing by outside. He continues to ventilate - the locals are not aligned to his way of life.

"They are all crazy. Crazy." And he ends with a resolve.

"But you have to accept people. That's life. I just get in my car and go fishing."

He blows smoke from his cigarette out through the open window and over the street. Little tobacco clouds lift into the warm summer night. The city simmers. And everyone floats into their dreams. I finish my beer as Patti Smith plays over the stereo. The barman drifts off while smoking; a gaze lost to the street outside.

Young Hustle

DARKNESS HAD NOW FALLEN across Tangier. After 11pm, the airy summer night has brought everyone out onto Boulevard Pasteur. It is Ramadan and Iftar has been served after the long day fasting. People walk off the evening feast with a celebratory flair. I went with the human flow, up Pasteur and on towards Café De Paris.

I immediately felt his focus on me. He stood off the flow, waiting for the easy touch to pass by. A shadow on my right-hand side just out of eyeshot; he followed me at an even pace. His approach came on soft feet. I slowed my pace slightly and he did the same. Then I glanced inward to see who was shadowing me. Once on my radar, he promptly kicked off his routine. A young face in jeans and a t-shirt, lanky, but with the look of street smarts. And so the dance began.

"Hey man, how are you this evening? Going for a walk?"

I smiled and focused ahead, picking up the pace; thinking a curt silence would steer his interest away.

"Are you looking for a restaurant? Where are you from? I can take you to a restaurant; it's just near here, up around the corner. I work there."

He flashed some old withered business cards in front of me. Somehow I didn't believe him.

He patiently pushed on with his routine. For him, it was about getting to the heart of the person; to open up that window of opportunity. I was now struggling to stay passive.

"What's your name? Where you from? Hey man, you're from England right?"

I flashed a brief smile and kept moving forward to the square ahead while ignoring him again. Place De Faro started to come into view. It was now a game of patience and the balance was quickly falling in his favour. He pushed on with the questions, patiently chipping away, while I start to crumble.

In the square, I could see my destination, the Café De Paris was in front of me. Trying to lose the young hustler in a matter of steps wasn't going to happen now. I took a seat on a concrete ledge overlooking the city. The dark bay of Tangier spread out below us.

He sat down next to me. Now things were getting too close for comfort. I turned to him.

"Hey, why don't you go and leave me alone please?" I asked.

Not exactly shaking in his boots, he smiled back confidently.

"We are all friends here man! I'm not here to hurt you! Look, there are police all around here."

He pointed with a grin to some uniforms wandering the square. I held steady, looking at families and couples passing by. I felt he was tiring somewhat; getting bored. I had become more awkward than beneficial. Well I felt awkward anyway, sitting there in suspended silence.

She was tall with long Saharan blonde hair and a skintight honey coloured dress. And she was crossing the square directly towards us. Her eyes sharply surveyed us. Her curves intimidated and a beautiful Middle Eastern flair took a seat to my left.

"Hi, have you got a light please?"

She held an unlit cigarette ready between her long fingers. Before I had a chance to reply the young hustler was on it. His face switched to a beaming delight.

"Hey, where you from?!" he asked her.

He leaned across in front of me and sparked her cigarette, eagerly talking like old friends reminiscing over a sneaky smoke. They continued to chat.

"I'm from Libya. Tripoli" she said smiling.

Then suddenly they both leaned back, switching to Arabic and continuing their exchange behind my back

Flanked by two young strangers late in the city centre of Tangier calls for some deep breathing. I looked out onto the passing traffic of Boulevard Pasteur. I was sensing a scam. And like a fleeting last minute display of sudden bizarre to my young hustler friend, I stood up and bolted for open road, through a crowd standing in a circle, off out of the square and onto the corner of Café De Paris. When I was out of view, I slipped in through one of the café's open doors. I retreated to the back, out of view from eyes on the street and the Place De Faro. I don't usually smoke, but calling for a packet with my order, I let off some steam with a cigarette and mint tea.

Local men took up every seat on the pavement outside the café, watching people pass where Boulevard Pasteur meets the roundabout of Place Du France. Comfortable couches seated people indoors for tea and coffee at brown tables. The surrounding walls curved and mirrored, make every part of the café visible. It is a scene that replicates the nineteen forties; a colonial life in North Africa.

A young woman takes a seat on her own at the back of the café near me. She orders a coffee. While waiting she looks directly at me in the mirror. She is partially obscured, with one eye visible. The waiters are classically dressed, straight out of the fifties, and serve waiting customers against a backdrop of brown leathered nostalgia. Fingers stroke her jet black hair, pushing it neatly behind her ear. Nail polish shines bright red. A confidence; a boldness with a subtle touch of elegance. I focus my attention on my mint tea and I light another cigarette.

One waiter greets a guest loudly in Arabic with a smile. They laugh together and the man takes a seat against the back wall. She has moved slightly. I can now clearly see her face. Brown hazel eyes and an oval beauty. Her shawl slowly drops and a neckline appears. I am still tensed up. The young hustler and mysterious lone Libyan had left me anxious. After removing my jacket, I called for another mint tea. I looked out through the windows of the café facing onto Place De Faro. No sign of the young hustler or the girl - just random reflections of passing light and darkness. Her eyes sparkled, her lips briefly parted and she let a modest smile slip. It was midnight in Tangier's Gran Café De Paris.

Eamonn Sheehy

In Through The Outdoor

IN THE EARLY MORNING I get into a petit taxi for the ferry terminal. The streets are empty and freshly sprinkled. The car speeds through narrow routes, down toward the port area. We stop at a roadblock directly in front of the terminal. And a complex it is, in every sense of the word. The whole port has gained size and muscle. Beefed up security, high reinforced railings, concrete slabbing. In the past, the port was just a walk off. No fences or barriers met the traveller who disembarked. From the ferry, it was an easy walk into the Kasbah. Now it represents another extension of that puzzling fortress phenomenon.

As I approached the entrance, everything started to become very European. Four border officials, a confident quadrant of control, sat by the entrance.

They looked me over the once and waved me through.

My passport ensures a smooth entry. The ferry rocks to-and-fro as the passengers flood on board. In the cabin, all mill around a snack bar getting teas and coffees. I take a seat by the window and settle back into its comfortable leather cradle. People roam aimlessly around me. Outside my window, I can see the port yard. It runs for a long distance off towards the Atlantic seaboard, until it meets first a metal fence, and then an awkward mound of giant boulders.

I see some boys on the boulders. A duo and another trio move separately along the perimeter. They watch the ferry as they move along over the boulders. A large uniformed man slowly walks out onto the wide concrete yard; a baton in hand. He stands looking up at the intruders. The boys keep low; heads down out of the sight. Of course the cameras have seen them. The man knows too. He sees some heads bob up curiously. He approaches with a wide brawny stance, chest out. The trio begin to back off, slipping between the boulders and out of the port area toward the main road. The man retreats back toward the enclosure of the terminal. And when he is gone, I spot the other group, the duo, emerge into view. Across the boulders, they take quick steps towards the water's edge, and a bit closer to our ferry.

And it's not just me watching. The surveillance system records every step. This is business after all.

Europe pays good money to Morocco, to reinforce its European border and keep refugees and migrants out. Authorities round them up and put them in detention centres. Sometimes truckloads of people are dropped in the scorching desert of the Maghreb away from any civilisation, in the hope they will just disappear and never come back.

The young men, some who are only teenage boys, are trying to move beyond that. The loud vibrating hum of the engine sends a shudder throughout the cabin. The roar runs across the terminal, signalling our departure. Their intention of getting on board the ferry with us to make the crossing seems almost imminent. The boys stare at our ferry while we pull away from the pier towards Europe.

Europe - the paranoid old man hiding behind a high wall; viewing, remote, divorced from reality. Europe with its apartment blocks of single moms, lonely men and hungry children. Europe - a massive expanse of land lacquered by concrete and connected by a maze of diseased tarmac arteries. Congested and unbreathable, with jagged edges patrolled by zombie men, uniformed and armed, pushing back the outside.

I never felt a current so gripping. The waves, like strips of steel, hit us over and over. The ferry bounces up and onward, forcing itself through the hard, heavy waters of the straits. I stagger from my seat to the back of the cabin and step out onto the deck for one last view. We pass small fishing boats that dance around us. Old Tangier glows proudly white in the background beyond them. A warm bleached stone metropolis, a place of acceptance, rising from the water to the hills. I see the silhouette of a young man standing on a high wall at the side of the port. The fading outline of a man barred from moving north.

The dreamers were still percolating in my mind. I imagine 'Man Boulevard Pasteur' settling down in an empty room of an empty building; his mattress serving as a release from exhaustion. Half broken, and in his greased up bomber jacket, he tumbles into his pillow with a groan, falling through to a deep sleep.

Young hustler struts the Boulevard, pacing himself between a fruitless future and dreams of young love. He continues with his routine, hoping for a break that leads somewhere good.

I imagine the old man hustler, rustling the wrinkles out of his newspaper in a local café; his brown cap tilted to the side on his head. Tea sits on the table and a friend across rants on, while a little granddaughter runs into the café, and happily swings from the bough of her grandfather's arm. The city simmers on. And Tangier begins to disappear amid the rising foam of waves.

Eamonn Sheehy

ABOUT THE AUTHOR

Eamonn Sheehy writes stories that jump into the deep side of travel, culture and counter-culture. His descriptive narratives portray vivid encounters with people living on the margins, across unique and unsettled regions. His work has appeared in YourMiddleEast.com, Kosovo 2.0 magazine, The Sarajevo Times and Redhorse Reporters.

Eamonn is from County Kerry in Ireland. He lives in a small village on the Cork coast along the South of Ireland's Wild Atlantic Way.

For more subversive nonfiction by this author go to
www.migratetothefringe.com

Summer In The City State

Migrate To The Fringe
2016

Made in the USA
Charleston, SC
11 October 2016